Kit Hill Sunset | Barry Gamble

One World Heritage Site: Ten Unique Areas

In 2006 selected mining landscapes across Cornwall and west Devon were inscribed as a UNESCO World Heritage Site, placing Cornish mining heritage on a par with international treasures like the Taj Mahal and the Great Wall of China. The largest industrial World Heritage Site in the UK, with over 20,000 hectares spread across Cornwall and west Devon, the Cornish Mining World Heritage Site offers myriad experiences to explore our world changing mining culture.

To understand the sheer magnitude of Cornish mining, one needs to explore the wider mining landscape, to look deep into its heart, reach back through time itself and unearth the stories of people whose mining culture shaped the world. Begin your journey to the heart and soul of Cornwall via the ten unique, diverse Areas that form the Cornish Mining World Heritage Site.

- Discover the 19 mining heritage visitor attractions

- Enjoy days out for the family, all year round

- Go underground for the real mining experience

- Share your experiences with us online, via Facebook, Twitter or Instagram, using the details below.

Share your experiences...

 Cornishmining

 @CornishMining

@CornishMining

Unn Tyller Ertach an Bys: Deg Tyller Unnik

Y'n vledhen 2006 tyleryow balweyth dewisys a-dreus Kernow ha Dewnens West a veu kovskrifys avel Tyller Ertach an Bys UNESCO, ow korra ertach balweyth kernewek orth an keth nivel ha tresoryow keswlasek kepar ha'n Taj Mahal ha Fos Veur China. An brassa Tyller Ertach an Bys diwysyansek y'n R U, ha dhodho moy ages 20,000 hektar lesys a-dreus Kernow ha Dewnens West, an

Tyller Ertach an Bys Balweyth Kernewek a brof prevyansow diniver rag hwithra agan gonisogeth valweyth a janjyas an bys.

Rag konvedhes braster pur balweyth kernewek yma edhom a hwithra tirwel ledanna balweyth, a vires yn town yn y golon, a dhehweles dres termyn y honan ha disynkleudhya hwedhlow tus ha dhedha gonisogeth valweyth a furvyas an bys. Dalethewgh agas viaj dhe golon hag enev Kernow der an deg Ranndir unnik ha divers a form an Tyller Ertach an Bys Balweyth Kernewek.

- Diskudhewgh an 19 tennvos balweyth rag godrigoryon

- Omlowenhewgh yn dedhyow yn-mes rag an teylu oll, dres an vledhen oll

- Kewgh yn-dann dhor rag prevyans balweyth gwir

- Kevrennewgh agas prevyansow genen warlinen, dre Facebook, Twitter po Instagram, ow tevnydhya an manylyon a-woles.

Un Sitio de Patrimonio de la Humanidad: diez áreas únicas

En el año 2006 diez áreas seleccionadas del paisaje minero a través de Cornualles y Devon fueron inscritas por la UNESCO como Patrimonio de la Humanidad, ubicando el patrimonio minero de Cornualles a la altura de maravillas del mundo como el Taj Mahal y la Gran Muralla China. Con más de 20.000 hectáreas distribuidas a través de Cornualles y el oeste de Devon, el Sitio de Patrimonio de la Humanidad de la Minería de Cornualles es el sitio de industrial Patrimonio de la Humanidad más vasto del Reino Unido y ofrece un gran número de actividades para explorar la cultura minera que transformó el mundo.

Para comprender la gran dimensión de la minería Cornuallesa es necesario explorar el paisaje minero en su conjunto, mirar en lo profundo de su corazón, retroceder en el tiempo y sacar a luz las historias de la gente cuya cultura minera transformó el mundo. Comience su viaje al corazón de Cornualles a través de las diez áreas exclusivas y diversas que constituyen el paisaje del Sitio de Patrimonio de la Humanidad de la Minería de Cornualles.

- Descubra las 19 atracciones mineras para visitantes.

- Disfrute de paseos para la familia durante todo el año.

- Descienda a una mina para vivir la verdadera experiencia minera.

- Comparta sus experiencias con nosotros en línea, a través de Facebook, Twitter o Instagram, utilizando los detalles a continuación.

Ein Weltkulturerbe:
zehn einzigartige Bereiche

Ausgewählte Landschaften in Cornwall und West Devon wurden 2006 als Unesco Weltkulturerbe anerkannt, wodurch Cornwalls Bergbauerbe auf eine Stufe mit internationalen Kulturschätzen wie dem Taj Mahal und der Chinesichen Mauer gestellt wurde. Als weiträumigstes Industrielle Weltkulturerbe im Vereinigten Königreich mit über 20.000 Hektar, verteilt über Cornwall und West Devon, bietet das Weltkulturerbe „Cornish Mining" unzählige Möglichkeiten, unsere Bergbaukultur, die die Welt verändert hat, zu erforschen.

Um das volle Ausmaß der Bedeutung des cornischen Bergbaus zu verstehen, ist es nötig, das Umfeld zu erkunden, tief in sein Herz zu sehen, die Zeit zurückzudrehen und die Geschichten der Menschen, deren Bergbaukultur die Welt geformt hat, ans Tageslicht zu bringen. Beginnen Sie Ihre Reise zum Herzen und der Seele von Cornwall über die zehn einzigartigen, mannigfaltigen Bereiche, die das Weltkulturerbe „Cornish Mining" bilden.

- Entdecken Sie die 19 Bergbau-Besucherattraktionen

- Erfreuen Sie sich an Tagesausfl ügen für die ganze Familie, das ganze Jahr hindurch

- Gehen Sie unter Tage für das authentische Bergbauerlebnis

- Teilen Sie Ihre Erfahrungen mit uns online, über Facebook, Twitter oder Instagram, mit den folgenden Details.

Dix domaines uniques,
un site du patrimoine mondial

En 2006, les paysages miniers sélectionnés à travers les Cornouailles et à l'ouest du Devon ont été inscrits sur la liste du patrimoine mondial de l'UNESCO, au même titre que le Taj Mahal et la Grande Muraille de Chine. Avec plus de 20.000 hectares, répartis sur les Cornouailles et à l'ouest du Devon, le site "Cornish Mining World Heritage" est le plus grand site industriel du patrimoine mondial au Royaume-Uni. Il off re de multiples expériences qui aident à mieux appréhender notre culture minière, un monde en mutation.

Pour comprendre l'ampleur de l'exploitation des mines des Cornouailles, il faut explorer plus largement son contexte historique, regarder attentivement ce paysage, remonter dans le temps, et déterrer les histoires des personnes qui, acteurs de cette culture minière, ont façonné ce monde. Commencez votre voyage au coeur des Cornouailles par ces dix domaines uniques, tous diff érents ; ils constituent le site Cornish Mining World Heritage, inscrit au patrimoine mondial de l'UNESCO.

- Découvrez les 19 attractions touristiques minières

- Profi tez de journées pour toute la famille, toute l'année

- Entrez dans la clandestinité pour une réelle expérience minière

- Partagez vos expériences avec nous en ligne, via Facebook, Twitter ou Instagram, en utilisant les détails ci-dessous.

Come and see how our mining culture shaped your world.

Experience the many wonders that lie waiting to be discovered here...

This is the story of Cornwall and west Devon's metal mining. It's a story of everyday people – hundreds of thousands of them – who had a profound effect on the landscape they lived in...and the world we live in today.

It's a story of danger; of men, women and children working in hazardous conditions to make a living. It's a story of incredible ingenuity; of discoveries and inventions that would change the world and influence the lives of future generations.

It's a story of tremendous community; of people sharing hardship and a sense of pride in their demanding work. It's a story of great wealth; of huge fortunes earned by a few, invested into magnificent houses and gardens filled with exotic plants collected from all over the world.

It's a story of change; of new towns and villages springing up and long lines of chimneys and engine houses punctuating the skyline.

It's a story set against one of the most spectacular backdrops you could imagine; the strikingly beautiful coastline, rugged moors, idyllic countryside, lush river valleys, bustling towns and harbours of Cornwall and west Devon.

This is the story of the Cornwall and West Devon Mining Landscape World Heritage Site; a tale that is as much about the people as the industry they worked in. The largest industrial World Heritage Site in the UK, it's a landscape of 20,000 hectares spread across Cornwall and west Devon, offering myriad experiences and opportunities to explore our world-changing mining culture.

This guide is designed to introduce you to some of those opportunities, suggesting ideas to help you 'investigate' this fascinating story and the iconic landscape that it created. It is not an exhaustive list of everything you can do in the Site (that would make for a very heavy book indeed!), but a taster of its vast potential to surprise and entertain you.

Botallack Arsenic Calciner | Ainsley Cocks

About **Cornish Mining**

What is a World Heritage Site?

Designated by the United Nations Educational, Scientific and Cultural Organization (UNESCO), World Heritage Sites are places of significance and value to the whole of humanity. This puts Cornish Mining on a par with international treasures like the Taj Mahal, the Pyramids, Stonehenge and the Great Wall of China.

Why is Cornish Mining a World Heritage Site?

Cornwall and west Devon's mining landscape, shaped during a period of intense industrial activity, is testimony to one of the greatest periods of economic, technological and social development Britain has ever known.

From 1700 to 1914, the metal mining industry played a vital role in transforming our way of life. It provided essential raw materials to feed the Industrial Revolution in Britain, and pioneered technological developments that helped shape the society we live in today. For example, Richard Trevithick's advances in steam engine technology – originally motivated by the need to pump water out of mines – ultimately enabled the development of steam trains, changing the world forever through the mass movement of people and goods.

This and other new engineering solutions and inventions developed here were exported to mining regions across the world – including Australia, the Americas and South Africa – playing a key role in the growth of an international capitalist economy. There are more than 175 places, across six continents, where Cornish mine workers took their skills, technology and traditions; A truly global heritage.

What metallic minerals were mined here?

A number of metals were mined in the region, but the 'big three' were:

- **Copper:** initial uses included the manufacture of coinage, to sheath and protect the hulls of British ships, the manufacture of the alloys brass and bronze, and for crucial machine bearings and fittings. Copper also became the essential metal of the electrical and communications industries.

- **Tin:** used in the early canning industry, for pewter ware (early plates, kettles and oil lamps) and to coat steel for tinplate. Also alloyed with copper to make bronze for machine bearings and ships' propellers.

- **Arsenic:** originally a by-product of copper and tin processing, arsenic was used extensively for dyes and pigments in the Lancashire cotton industry and for printing. Later became an essential insecticide, helping control the Colorado Beetle and Boll Weevil which devastated crops in America.

What happened to Cornish Mining?

Increasing competition through the expanding global mining industry was to reduce metal prices significantly during the latter 19th century, eventually forcing many local producers to close. This led to a significant increase in economic migration, a process which had commenced in the early decades of the 19th century as mine workers used their much valued skills to work in mines elsewhere in Britain and around the globe. Cornwall alone is thought to have lost between 250,000 and 500,000 people from around 1815 to 1915, a movement defined today as 'The Great Migration'. Today it is estimated there are over six million people worldwide descended from migrant Cornish.

What is there to see within the Site?

Ten separate Areas make up the World Heritage Site. Each has its own character, opportunities for adventure, and a different combination of the features that make up the Cornish Mining landscape.

The World Heritage Site has recorded over 200 Cornish type engine houses within its boundaries, the largest concentration of these industrial icons anywhere in the world. But Cornish Mining is about far more than mine sites – the mining industry impacted on all aspects of life. Many of our towns and villages were either transformed by a growing industrial population or newly built to house them. They reveal their history in the rows of distinctive terraced cottages, shops, chapels and substantial public buildings. Today you'll find plenty of great cafés, pubs, restaurants, art galleries, and museums.

The remains of the transport networks that were developed to serve the mines during the early 19th century – the railways, mineral tramways, canals, ports and quays – can now be explored by foot, bicycle or boat, making for invigorating and fascinating days out. And within the Site, several of Cornwall's great houses and gardens – paid for with the profits of the mining industry – now open their doors to visitors.

Cornish Mining
World Heritage Site

Ten separate 'Areas' make up the Cornish Mining World Heritage Site.

Each has its own character, opportunities for adventure, and a different combination of the features that make up the Cornish Mining landscape.

The maps in this guide give an indication of where the featured locations are. For more detail, refer to the relevant Ordnance Survey map - we've noted which is best for each Area within the Cornish Mining World Heritage Site.

01 St Just
Mining on the edge of the earth

03 Tregonning & Gwinear
Diverse landscapes and great houses

Glossary:
A brief description of mining terms used in this guide, highlighted in **pink** throughout the book.

A, a

Adit
From the Latin Aditus – an entry; a horizontal or slightly sloping tunnel driven for access or drainage purposes whereby water could drain away by gravity without the need for pumping. These were also used for exploration purposes in the development of early mines, as when driven on lode outcrops from the bases of sea cliffs.

Aluvial deposits (tin)
Detrital ores - that which have been eroded and transported from the originating mineral lode by water action and redeposited in the beds of water courses, thereby forming the concentrated tin ground; this being subsequently worked by **Tin streaming**.

B, b

Bal or Ball
From Cornish 'Pal' a shovel, and hence 'a digging' (a mine). Generally applied to a group of individual workings which frequently became incorporated into a single large mine. See also **Wheal.**

Beam engine
A type of steam-engine much favoured in Cornwall, west Devon and elsewhere, used for pumping, winding and the crushing of ores preparatory to dressing. The power from a large cylinder set vertically in an engine-house was transferred via a massive rocking beam or bob to the pumps in the shaft outside. For winding and crushing, the bob was instead attached to a flywheel and crank on a loading next to the bob-wall (or in the case of all indoor engines, the side wall). In most cases, the engine house formed an integral part of the framing of the engine.

C, c

Calciner
A furnace and heating chamber in which ores were roasted to remove impurities such as sulphur and arsenic. These were also known as Burning Houses, later patterns being of reverberatory design. The Brunton pattern calciner, introduced in the mid-nineteenth century, was mechanically powered, and operated on a continuous basis, unlike earlier designs. Other patterns of calciner were also devised, the majority named after their designers (e.g. Oxland, Hocking and Loam).

Consols
A shortened form of the term 'consolidated', used where a number of mines were brought together and worked under a common management, e.g. Devon Great Consols.

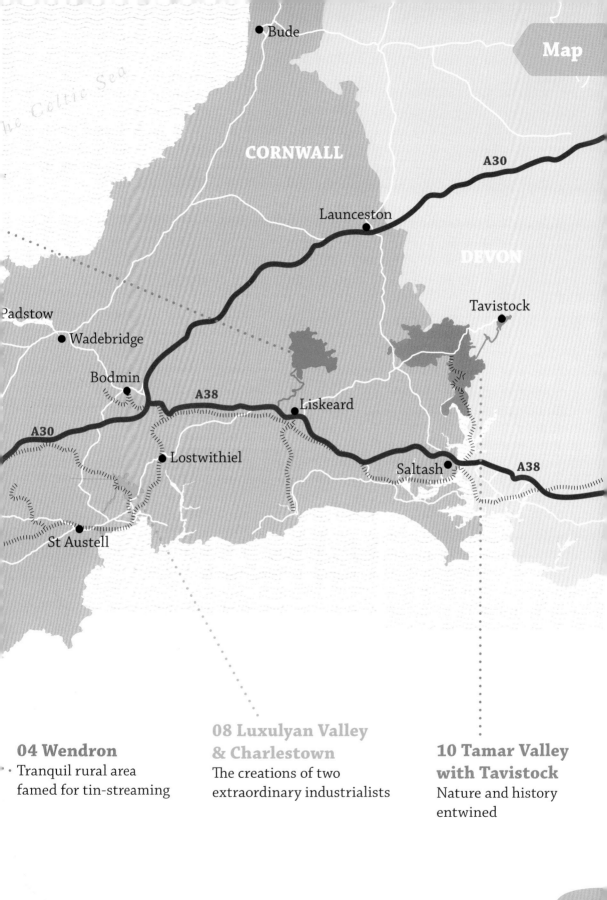

The Celtic Sea

Bude

CORNWALL

A30

Launceston

DEVON

Tavistock

Padstow

Wadebridge

Bodmin

A38

Liskeard

A30

Lostwithiel

Saltash

A38

St Austell

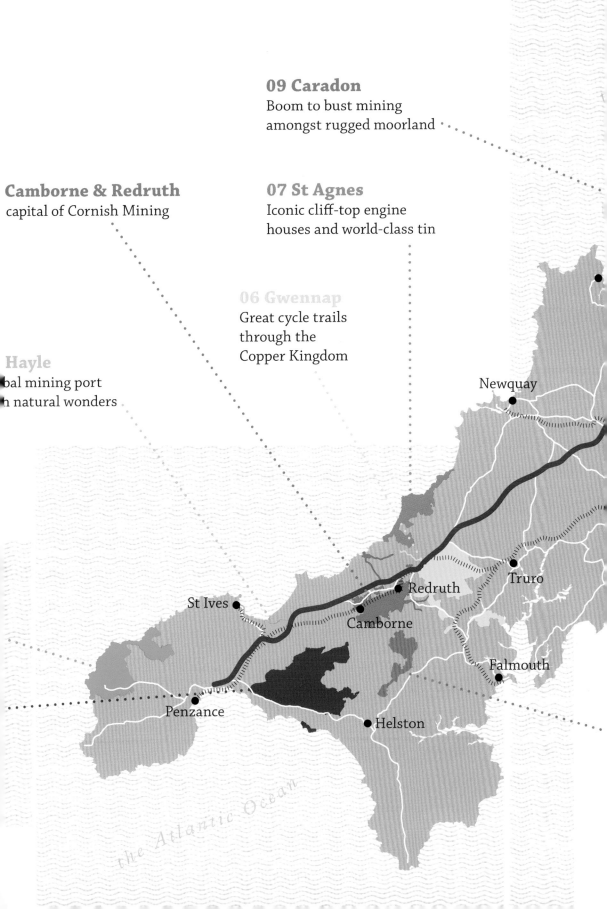

09 Caradon
Boom to bust mining
amongst rugged moorland

Camborne & Redruth
capital of Cornish Mining

07 St Agnes
Iconic cliff-top engine
houses and world-class tin

06 Gwennap
Great cycle trails
through the
Copper Kingdom

Hayle
bal mining port
h natural wonders

Newquay

Truro

Redruth

St Ives

Camborne

Falmouth

Penzance

Helston

the Atlantic Ocean

Dressing Floors

An (often extensive) area at surface on a mine where the various processes of concentration of ore took place - these consisted of crushing or stamping to attain a uniform size range, sizing (particularly on later mines), separation of waste rock, concentration (generally mechanically and hydraulically on tin mines, manually on copper mines), the removal of contaminant minerals (by calcination, flotation, magnetic separation), and finally drying and bagging for transportation to the smelter. Tin floors in particular were generally laid out down a slope to reduce mechanical or manual handling between stages in the process.

Dump or Burrow

(alternatively spoil heap, spoil dump, spoil tip) A pile of waste material, usually from a mine or quarry. May contain primary waste (where this could not be disposed of underground) or waste from various stages in the dressing process.

Engine House

A building designed to contain steam, gas, oil or electric engines on a mine or other works. From the eighteenth to early twentieth centuries, usually a robust masonry construction of three floors over a cataract pit to accommodate a vertical cylinder **beam engine**. Houses of this type were used to contain pumping, winding and stamping engines, with the former types usually arranged in a right-angle about a principal shaft. The sturdy build has led to many examples surviving into the twenty-first century in Cornwall and west Devon and their presence in the landscape has become an iconic representation of the importance of metal mining to south-west Britain.

Flue

A masonry-constructed tunnel or conduit connecting a furnace to a chimney stack.

Foundry

A manufacturing site where metals are cast or formed to create machine parts, tools, and civic or domestic ironwork.

Grist

Grain or quantity of grain for grinding into wheat or corn meal.

Leat

An artificial water-course, built to carry a supply of water to a mine or around it.

Lode

A linear zone of mineralization underground, referred to as a vein, rake or seam in other parts of Britain. Generally vertical or near-vertical, and often extending for considerable distances along its trend.

Open-Cast

An excavation whereby the mineral lode or lodes are opened to the surface and exploited directly, in a manner similar to stone quarrying.

Ore

A mineral or mixture of minerals which could be worked for sale.

Scoria

A dark coloured slag formed as a waste by-product of the copper smelting process; saw limited use in the early 1800s as a building material when cast as blocks; eg the Black Bridge, Hayle.

Shaft

A vertical or near-vertical tunnel sunk within a mine for pumping, hoisting, ventilation, access or other purposes.

Smallholdings

Small plots of land, usually from 3-5 acres (1-2 hectares) in extent, which were leased to mine workers and others on which to build a cottage and lay out fields for subsistence.

Smelting

The process whereby mineral ores are subjected to heat in combination with chemical reducing agents in a furnace, to liberate base or precious metals for sale.

Stamps

A mechanical device for crushing ore-bearing rock to a fine sand. Heavy vertically-mounted beams (or later iron rods) carrying cast or forged iron heads were sequentially lifted and dropped onto the prepared ore beneath them by a series of cams mounted on a rotating drum; this usually being driven by a water-wheel or rotative steam engine.

Tin Dressing

The concentration of tin ores contained in rock excavated from the working areas of a mine. See **Dressing Floors**.

Tin Streaming (streamwork)

An area worked for detrital (re-deposited) tin deposits by shallow excavation; often characterised by linear dumps, river diversion, and evidence for **Leats**. Some such works (dryworks) exploited deposits of shoad in now dry valleys and on hillsides, where concentrations of this material were economically workable. Leats and reservoirs were necessary to work these sites, and are characteristic of them. This term is also often applied to tin recovery works where tin ore lost with waste discharged from mine **Dressing Floors** into water courses is recovered for sale by third parties.

Tramway

A method of transportation for ore and materials at surface using iron plates or rails; similar to a modern railway and operated using either horse or locomotive power; also known as tramroads.

Water Wheel

Wheel fitted with buckets or paddles around its periphery, and driven by the weight or force of a stream of water directed onto them.

Wheal also **Whele, While, Huel**

Dialect variations of a Cornish term for a mine working. See **Bal**.

The Cornish Mining World Heritage Site Areas

Geevor Mine - Victory Shaft headframe | Barry Gamble

Mining on **the edge of the earth**

A stone's throw from Land's End, this is the most westerly Area of the Site. An exposed landscape scoured by the elements, St Just is characterised by big skies, jagged rocks, stark moorland, and iconic cliff-top engine houses perched in some incredible locations – no wonder this dramatic setting has inspired generations of artists, writers and photographers. World-famous for their mineralogy, the mining sites here are extremely well preserved, as is the sense of community amongst the people whose lives they once dominated.

Mining Heritage

This Area's unique geography and mineralogy led to the development of the largest concentration of undersea tin and copper mines anywhere in the world in the 18th and 19th centuries. At Levant Mine, the undersea workings extended over a mile out to sea, at a depth of around half a mile beneath the seabed. The oldest surviving Cornish **beam engine** (c.1840) remains in its original house here – it has been restored, and still works under steam. Geevor, one of the last mines to close in Cornwall (1990), was saved from demolition and is now the largest metalliferous mine site open to the public in the UK. Three stream valleys in this Area also contain some of the best-preserved water-powered tin **stamping mills** anywhere in the Site.

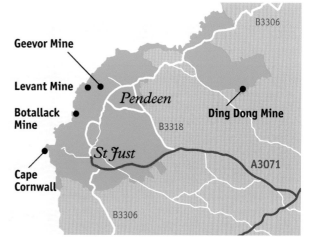

You'll hear the boom of waves crashing onto the jagged cliffs and swirling between the rocks below

Storm at Crowns, Botallack
Barry Gamble

Practicalities

Getting there • St Just is seven miles from Penzance. By car, follow the **A3071** from Penzance or the **B3306** from St Ives. The **7, 18C, 240, 409** and **A17** bus services all serve St Just, as well as the popular **Atlantic Coaster** open-top service, which runs along the spectacular B3306 coast road from St Ives from May. See **firstgroup.com/cornwall** for timetables. The nearest mainline train station is **Penzance.** See **nationalrail.co.uk** for the latest information

Suggested map • **Ordnance Survey map 102** - Land's End, Penzance and St Ives (Explorer Maps)

Dog friendliness • The St Just Area has lots of year-round dog-friendly beaches, including Progo, Porthnaven and Portheras Cove. Inland, keep dogs on leads on farmland with grazing animals

Parking • There are free car parks in St Just and Pendeen while Geevor has a large free visitor car park. There are National Trust car parks at Cape Cornwall and Botallack

Public toilets • By the car parks in St Just, Pendeen and Cape Cornwall

Eating & drinking • St Just has lots of good cafés and pubs. On Market Square, Kegen Teg is a lovely café serving delicious wholesome food. The Cook Book on Cape Cornwall Street serves cream teas, scrumptious cakes and light lunches, and has a fascinating second-hand bookshop upstairs. The 14th century King's Arms Inn is an atmospheric spot for a drink or a meal, while in Pendeen, the North and Radjel Inns are also worthy of a visit. The café at Geevor has a stunning view, and can be used without paying the site admission fee

Picnic spots • Watch Croft, Lafrowda Common, Ding Dong and Kenidjack Head have panoramic views across the Area (but can be quite windy!), or find a sheltered spot along the spectacular coast path. Please help us to look after the World Heritage Site by taking all rubbish away with you

St Just is a prime example of an industrial mining town, with its distinctive cottage rows, Methodist chapels, hotels, pubs, shops and civic buildings. At Porthledden, Cape Cornwall, the grand former residence of Captain Francis Oats (one-time Chair of De Beers) dominates the hillside, reflecting the wealth he earned while mining diamonds in South Africa.

Discover...

Industry

The coast path links most of the principal mine sites, which lie on a spectacular four-mile stretch of coastline. Park at Cape Cornwall and join the coast path heading north-east to take in Kenidjack Head (the stream here once powered up to 50 water wheels), Wheal Edward Zawn, Botallack (where you can visit the Botallack Count House and see displays telling you more about mining on this coast), Levant Mine and Beam Engine, and Trewellard Zawn.

Nature

Take a stroll up on the moors around Ding Dong Mine, and you're likely to see buzzards, jackdaws, skylarks and ravens circling in the skies above. On the ground, look out for rabbits and the wildflowers, heather and gorse that blanket the moors in the spring and summer.

Times past

At the heart of St Just, just off Bank Square, is the Plen an Gwary, a grassed amphitheatre that is one of only two surviving medieval amphitheatres in Cornwall. It's been used as a theatre, sports arena (once famous for Cornish wrestling and hand rock drilling competitions) and meeting place for the nearby mining communities.

Highlights

Watch the waves crashing on the rocks below the Crowns engine houses at Botallack, which are perched on a narrow promontory just above the sea

Experience the solitude of Ding Dong, a remote Cornish engine house sitting high up on the treeless moors that is surrounded by the remains of mine workers' cottages and fields. The views towards Mounts Bay from here are truly breathtaking

Walk around the beautiful Cape Cornwall – Britain's only cape – where an ornate solitary mine stack stands sentinel on the coast

Explore the town of St Just, with its characteristic rows of granite mine workers' cottages, public squares, shops, cafés, art galleries, and historic outdoor performance space—the Plen an Gwary or 'playing place'

Take a tour of Geevor Tin Mine – one of the last Cornish mines to close, it is one of only a few mine sites with extensive collections of machinery open to the public in Cornwall. The imposing headframe at Victory Shaft can be seen from miles around

See Levant Mine, which is spectacularly sited on the cliff edge. Its beam engine has been restored by the Greasy Gang, and is driven by steam again

Explore the Tin Coast, visit **https://tin-coast. net** to learn how you can discover the rich mining history of the Area

Did you know?
Cornish migrants introduced rugby, pasties and saffron cake to South Africa

Cape Cornwall | Barry Gamble

Hayle Harbour | Barry Gamble

Global mining port with **natural wonders**

Taking its name from heyl, the Cornish word for estuary, this Area is dominated by water: rivers, pools, sluicing ponds, quays, wharves, and, of course, the sea. Huge sand dunes lie between the town and the beautiful St Ives Bay, with the dark hills of the West Penwith Moors looming to the west. In the early 19th century, Hayle was the most important mining port and steam engine manufacturing centre in the world. Despite its decline, today's lively communities buzz with the prospect of imminent regeneration. Here you'll find plenty of signs of the town's great past, along with beautiful beaches stretching out under vast skies.

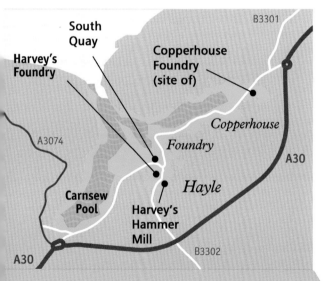

At low tide, you'll smell the seaweed that clings to the harbour walls and wharves

Mining Heritage

Hayle's proximity to the major copper and tin mines of Redruth and Camborne gave this Area an important role. As a key sea port, Hayle not only had vital links with South Wales and the Swansea copper smelters but also reached out to the far corners of the world – Cornish **beam engines** built here were exported for use across four continents. Hayle's harbour quays cover a large area and give an idea of the scale of industrial activity which took place here during the 19th century.

Carnsew Pool | Barry Gamble

Cockle Bank, Hayle | Adam Sharpe

Practicalities

Getting there • Hayle is just off the **A30**, nine miles south-east of St Ives (by car – shorter as the crow flies!). By bus, **First's T1** route runs via Truro, Camborne, Redruth, Hayle and Penzance. See **firstgroup.com/cornwall** for timetables. By train, Hayle is on the main London to Penzance line, but you will need to change at St Erth if travelling from St Ives. See **nationalrail.co.uk** for the latest information

Suggested map • **Ordnance Survey map 102**: Land's End, Penzance and St Ives (Explorer Maps)

Dog friendliness • Hayle has three, year-round, dog friendly beaches at Mexico, Upton and Peter's Point beaches. There is a dog ban from Easter Day to 1st October on Hayle Towans beach, between the Hayle River and Black Cliffs

Parking • There are Pay & Displays at Foundry Square, Commercial Road and in the Towans (look for signs as some clampers operate here)

Public toilets • Gwithian Towans Toilets are open Easter to 30th September and October half-term holiday

Eating & drinking • Sample a famous Philps' pasty, or relax in the stylish and comfortable Salt Bar & Kitchen in Foundry Square. Mr B's artisan ice cream parlour has over 20 different flavours of scrumptious ice cream

Picnic spots • Hayle has three miles of sandy beach, and there are plenty of great spots to be found among the dunes and low cliffs. Please help us to look after the World Heritage Site by taking all rubbish away with you

Two of the most important iron foundries in the Site were here, as well as the largest copper **smelter**, a shipyard, flour and **grist mills**, a gasworks, and a brewery. A fierce and long-running rivalry grew between the competing foundries (Harvey's and that of the Cornish Copper Company), as they argued over access to the sea. This contributed to the development of Foundry and Copperhouse as individual settlements, located around the sites of these two companies.

The copper smelting process generated large amounts of waste slag, which was cast into blocks and used as a building material. Many buildings in the town display these characteristic dark-coloured blocks, known as **Scoria.**

Harvey's Foundry Barn | Ainsley Cocks

Discover...

Industry

Cross the railway swing bridge and follow the estuary to the sea, looking out for the remains of wharf side industry including the extensive quays, sluice gates and sluicing ponds.

Nature

Carnsew Pool is a designated Site of Special Scientific Interest (SSSI) for its importance for nature conservation, especially birds. Walk across the granite wharf of South Quay, find a comfortable spot and get your binoculars out!

Times past

Explore the back roads and paths around the Foundry area, to find the impressive villas and ornate townhouses of the industry's managers tucked away from the hustle and bustle.

Highlights

Cross the railway swing bridge (1877) and follow the estuary, through the old harbour and wharfside, and past the dunes to the huge sandy expanse of Gwithian Beach beyond

Spot the many different types of birds to be found around Carnsew Pool, a Site of Special Scientific Interest (SSSI)

Follow the King George V Memorial Walk from Phillack, taking in the pretty gardens around Copperhouse Pool, and look out for Black Bridge (built from Scoria Blocks made from the waste slag produced by copper ore smelting at nearby Copperhouse)

Watch the sunset over the old harbour, with the towering dunes and St Ives in the background

Explore the area around Foundry Barn, and imagining it in its booming, busy heyday

Visit Hayle Heritage Centre located at the historic site of Harvey's Foundry and view exhibitions on Hayle's rich industrial history. The Harvey's Foundry Trust runs a variety of workshops, temporary exhibitions, guided tours and community events. Visit **hayleheritagecentre.org.uk** for more information

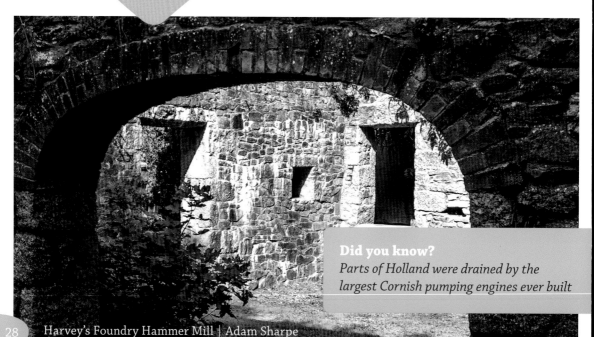

Did you know?
Parts of Holland were drained by the largest Cornish pumping engines ever built

Harvey's Foundry Hammer Mill | Adam Sharpe

Diverse landscapes **and great houses**

The largest of the ten Areas, Tregonning and Gwinear contains some of the most diverse landscapes in the whole Site. Ranging from the idyllic pastoral charms of the rural farmland in the west of the Area to the atmospheric cliffscapes at Rinsey – with silent woods, exposed hills and subtropical gardens in between – it is vast, historic and remarkable. Two great houses and their estates – Godolphin and Clowance – define the Area, providing a valuable insight into the wealth of some of Cornwall's most successful industrialists and mine owners.

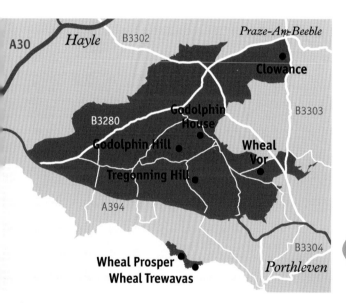

Great Wheal Fortune, near the former mining town of Breage, is an exceptional example of a surviving **open-cast** tin mine. Some sources also suggest this area was the first to have seen the use of both a Savery pump (around 1700) and a Newcomen atmospheric pumping engine (around 1710-16), although evidence for this is uncertain.

> If you're lucky, you may hear the loud, ringing call of Cornish Choughs on the cliff-tops

Mining Heritage

Much of this Area's mining history focuses on and around Godolphin; a district of early tin mines can be found within the former boundaries of the estate - areas now used for farming. These include Wheal Vor, which at its peak in the 1830s employed over 1,100 people and was the richest tin mine in Cornwall.

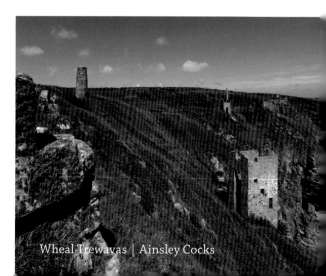

Wheal Trewavas | Ainsley Cocks

Practicalities

Getting there • Godolphin House and Rinsey are both within five miles of Helston. **First's U4** bus travels to Porthleven and Praa Sands (Wheal Trewavas and Prosper are between the two), and there are regular buses into Helston town centre. See **firstgroup.com/cornwall**

Suggested map • **Ordnance Survey Explorer maps 103** (The Lizard, Helston and Falmouth) **and 102** (Land's End, Penzance and St Ives)

Dog friendliness • Godolphin has lots of great walks around the estate. Rinsey headland is grassy and popular, but the nearby cove and Praa Sands do not allow dogs from Easter Day to 1st October

Parking • Rinsey has a National Trust car park (good for access to Wheal Prosper), and there is National Trust parking at Godolphin

Public toilets • Toilet facilities can be found at Godolphin

Eating & drinking • Porthleven has The Corner Deli for sandwiches and pizzas with locally sourced produce, as well as a number of welcoming pubs and restaurants. For its size, Praze-An-Beeble has good amenities, including a great local pub serving food

Picnic spots • The entire stretch of coast around Rinsey is perfect for picnicking, as is the expansive grassland in and around Tregonning Hill and the Godolphin Estate

To the south of the site, two undersea copper mines (Wheal Trewavas and Prosper) near Rinsey offer a unique glimpse of how treacherous mining could be. Trewavas, which seems to burst out of the cliff-edge, is particularly inspiring. Its neighbour, Wheal Prosper, sits a little further along the cliff and both sites have now been conserved by the National Trust.

Godolphin House | Ainsley Cocks

Wheal Prosper | Ainsley Cocks

Discover...

Industry

Explore the cliffs around Wheal Prosper and Wheal Trewavas, some of the most strikingly situated engine houses in the Site. If you're lucky you might even see an RNAS Culdrose helicopter performing training exercises nearby.

Nature

Go for a walk around the woodland areas that stretch out west from Godolphin, where much of the landscape remains unchanged from when mining was Cornwall's main trade. The woods are rich with wildlife throughout the year, and positively burst with bluebells and birdsong in the spring.

Times past

Park at and explore Praze-An- Beeble. Still reminiscent of its mining heyday, the village has lines of mine workers' cottages and surrounding countryside dotted with **smallholdings.**

Highlights

Take in the breathtaking sights and sounds of Wheal Trewavas and Wheal Prosper – some of the best-known undersea mines, they are perched dramatically on the edge of rugged cliffs

---

Visit Godolphin House, once home to some of Cornwall's most successful mine owners, and exploring its gardens that are thought to date from the late Middle Ages

---

Enjoy the panoramic views from Tregonning and Godolphin Hills that can stretch as far as St Agnes and Hayle on a clear day

---

Explore the beautiful Rinsey headland and beach (at low tide), and nearby Porthleven (not in the Site), with its spectacular harbour that sweeps right into the centre of the village

---

Did you know?
The Godolphin Arabian was one of three thoroughbreds from which most modern racehorses are descended

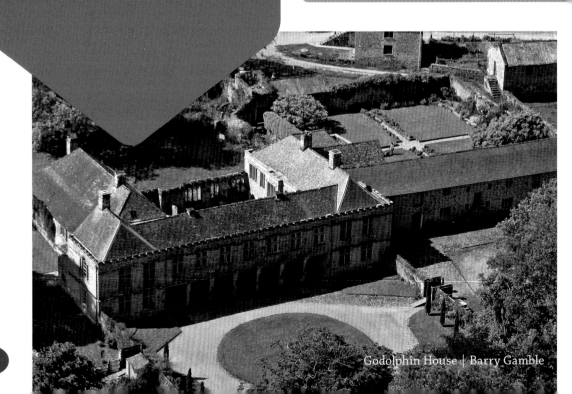

Godolphin House | Barry Gamble

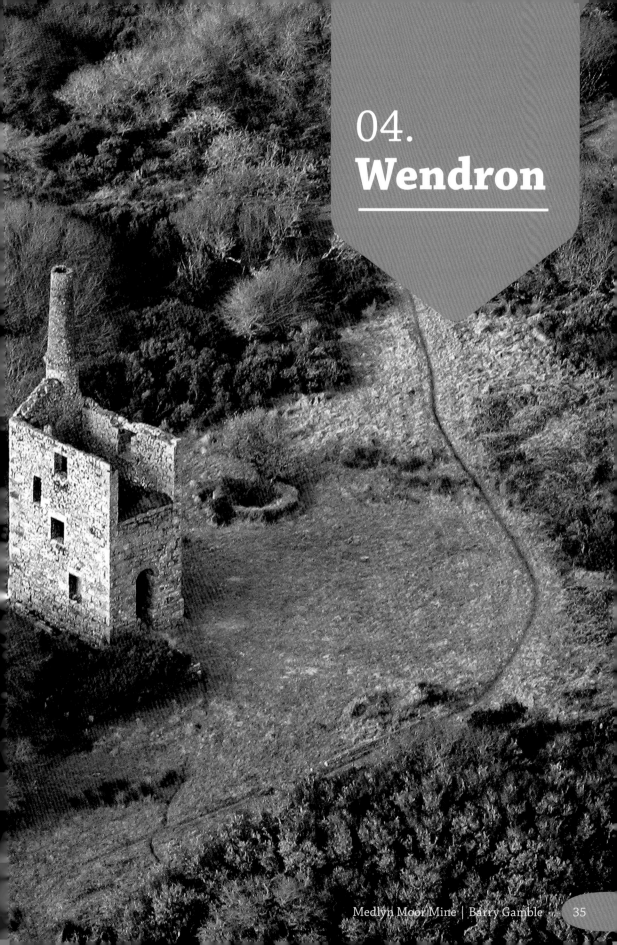

04.
Wendron

Tranquil rural area famed
for tin-streaming

In the heart of beautiful countryside surrounded by open moorland and gushing streams, Wendron is one of the smallest Areas in the Site – although its rich tin deposits meant it once had enough inhabitants to rival the combined population of Redruth and Camborne. This demand led to the creation of a large number of smallholdings around Carnmenellis, which are among the best preserved in the entire Site. Here you can see pretty granite cottages and tiny fields framed by dozens of low walls made from cob and moorland granite respectively.

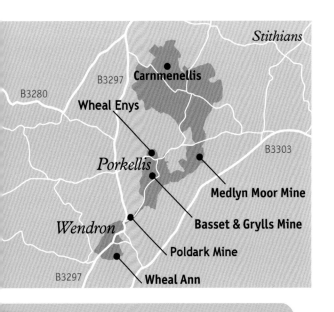

Stithians

B3297 **Carnmenellis**

B3280

Wheal Enys

Porkellis

B3303

Medlyn Moor Mine

Wendron

Basset & Grylls Mine

Poldark Mine

B3297

Wheal Ann

Mining Heritage

Deep-shaft mines had become established here by the 17th century, but, before this, tin was extracted by **tin-streaming**. Wendron was arguably one of the most productive areas for this, and records indicate the district's rich **alluvial deposits** were worked by tin-streamers from before the 1500s. The discovery of mortar stones (used to crush tin ore, probably sourced from the nearby River Cober), and hand-cut (rather than gunpowder driven) shallow levels at Poldark Mine (Wheal Roots), confirm the long history of tin working at this location.

High above, skylarks and crows play in the mine buildings and treetops, while rabbits and squirrels rustle in the long grass and undergrowth around Porkellis Moor

Porkellis Moor Pool | Barry Gamble

Wheal Ann | Adam Sharpe

Practicalities

Getting there • Wendron village is situated on the **B3297**, roughly two miles north of Helston. Poldark Mine is close by, and Carnmenellis is accessible via Four Lanes, near Redruth

Suggested map • **Ordnance Survey map 103**: The Lizard, Falmouth & Helston (Explorer Maps)

Dog friendliness • Most footpaths, Public Rights of Way and open spaces in this Area allow dogs. Dogs are not permitted at Poldark mine

Parking • Cars can park at Stithians Lake in the north-east of the Area, and Wendron has a small number of spaces in the village centre. Poldark Mine has a visitor car park

Public toilets • There are toilet facilities for visitors at Poldark Mine and for customers at The New Inn in Wendron village centre

Eating & drinking • Food is served at The New Inn (which was built using local granite from the 18th century). The Star Inn at Porkellis is a cosy local pub serving food

Picnic spots • Much of this Area is accessible by public footpaths, so there are many places to stop and enjoy the scenery. On a sunny day, Stithians Lake is a hive of activity and is great for watching sailing boats and windsurfers. Please help us to look after the World Heritage Site by taking all rubbish away with you

Underground at Poldark the unique experience of going deep into a real mine gives you the miner's perspective

These early tin works led to the discovery of mineral lodes, which were exploited through both shallow and deep-shaft mining from the 17th century onwards. The small number of surviving engine houses are important landmarks – particularly those at Wheal Ann, Trumpet Consols and Wheal Enys.

Underground at Wheal Roots, Poldark Mine | Richard Williams

Discover...

Mining

Take a walking tour around the mine sites of Wheal Enys, Porkellis Moor, Wheal Ann and Basset & Grylls, which are all near Wendron village. Basset & Grylls was the scene of tragedy in 1858, when a surface pond collapsed straight into the mine, killing seven local workers.

Nature

The shallow, low land at Porkellis Moor yielded its metallic treasures long before **shaft** mining reached its peak, and the evidence of this can still be found in the landscape today, hidden amongst the gorse and heath grasses.

Times past

The surviving **smallholdings** at Carnmenellis are characteristic of the Area. Created to meet the demands of the mining and quarrying workforce, the **smallholdings** forged an important link between the extractive industries and farming that is still relevant today.

Highlights

Venture down into Wheal Roots – the 18th century tin mine at Poldark – to learn about Cornish mining history and find out what conditions were actually like for Cornish mine workers

Also, see the re-sited Greensplat steam beam engine, believed to have been the last to pump commercially in Cornwall

Explore Porkellis Moor, a Cornwall Wildlife Trust reserve, where nature has reclaimed the ancient mining landscape

Walk the footpaths around Carnmenellis (in the north of the Area) and see the surviving mine workers' smallholdings – probably the best examples in the whole Site. (Footpaths ring Carnmenellis but do not connect with the summit of the hill)

Did you know?
Cornish mine workers introduced football to Mexico

Smallholdings, Carnmenellis | Barry Gamble

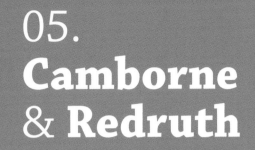

05.
Camborne & Redruth

The capital of **Cornish mining**

This was the centre of the Cornish mining industry, and home to many of its most important mines and individuals. The impressive bulk of Carn Brea – a high granite ridge with jagged outcrops and fantastic 360° vistas – frames most views of Camborne and Redruth, serving as a reminder of the geology that underpinned their rapid growth. Featuring essential rail links to Portreath harbour, historic mining cottages, the Great Flat Lode (an extensive flat-dipping mineral vein extremely rich in tin), and South Crofty, Cornwall's last mine to produce tin, this Area includes rugged open countryside, a lovely sandy beach, and bustling towns with the remains of its mining history ever-present.

Mining Heritage

Between roughly 1770 and 1920, Camborne and Redruth was the most populated and innovative metal mining district in the entire Site, with some of Cornwall's richest, deepest and most famous copper and tin mines. A slump in copper prices had hit the Area hard, but thanks to the discovery of tin in the Great Flat Lode (1870), the mining workforce were able to find employment in some of the most significant tin mines of the late 19th century.

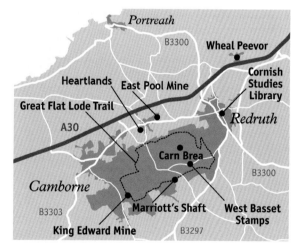

Mines such as Wheal Uny, South Wheal Frances and Wheal Grenville soon became renowned for the immense amount of tin being produced. The steep rise in output also sustained important rail transport links – particularly to Devoran and Point along the Redruth & Chasewater Railway, which supplied coal essential for the mines' many engines. The Area also saw the establishment of King Edward Mine in 1897, previously a training school for the world renowned Camborne School of Mines, the site is now a fascinating visitor attraction.

The Camborne and Redruth Mining District became significant internationally for the pioneering technological progress made here, such as Richard Trevithick's steam engines, William Bickford's invention of the safety fuse (which saved countless miners' lives), and William Murdoch's house, being the first in the world to be lit by gas (in 1792). A visit to the Cornish Studies Library (Redruth) and East Pool Mine (Pool) will tell you the story of this Area and its huge achievements. From 2019 the Library will be housed at Kresen Kernow, Cornwall's new archive centre.

The Puffing Devil, East Pool Mine

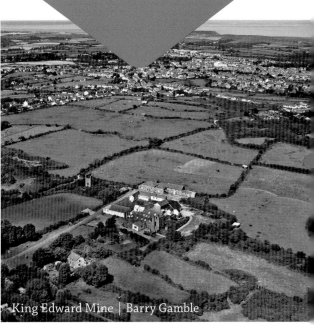

The Great Flat Lode is classic Cornish mining landscape, with the largest number of Cornish type engine houses anywhere in the Site.

Did you know?
Richard Trevithick road-tested the world's first practical steam powered vehicle in Camborne (1801)

Practicalities

Getting there • Both Camborne and Redruth have train stations on the main London to Penzance line, and are situated just off the **A30**. Portreath is close to both (roughly four miles to the north), and is on the coast. There are regular buses to Redruth and Camborne from most major Cornish areas (**T1** and **T2** via Truro), and buses to Portreath also run from Truro, Camborne and Redruth. See **firstgroup.com/cornwall** for more information

Suggested map • **Ordnance Survey map 104**: Redruth & St Agnes (Explorer Maps)

Dog friendliness • Dogs are allowed around most of the mining sites, including the Great Flat Lode. Portreath Beach has a dog ban between Easter and 1st October

Parking • There are numerous car parks in Redruth, Carn Brea and Camborne, and along the Great Flat Lode at Marriott's shaft and West Basset. Portreath also has a good sized car park above the beach

Public toilets • Both Redruth and Camborne's town centres have toilet facilities. Portreath beach also has public toilets. There are also toilets at Heartlands

King Edward Mine | Barry Gamble

Eating & drinking • Redruth and Camborne have lots of traditional bakeries, cafés and pubs, they also have restaurants with food ranging from fine dining to pub food. Portreath beach has a range of locally-sourced cafés and restaurants. Heartlands has a café based in the old Carpenter's Workshop with beautiful wooden beam ceiling and original features offering fresh local food served within a real community hub

Picnic spots • Many of the mine areas around Redruth and Camborne are potential picnic spots, and Portreath has a lovely beach which is perfect on calm days. Please help us to look after the World Heritage Site by taking all rubbish away with you

South Wheal Frances with smallholdings | Ainsley Cocks

Discover...

Mining

Rent bikes and try out the excellent cycle trail around the Great Flat Lode (try **cornwallbikehire.co.uk**). The trail, which is generally easy-going, stops off at key industrial locations and has numerous panels with information about the mines along the way. You can also cycle along the Mineral Tramways Coast to Coast route to Portreath, which also passes through a number of significant mining sites.

Look out for the Redruth International Mining and Pasty Festival held each September with local market stalls, local entertainment and lots of pasties!

Nature

Walking along the headland around Portreath, you'll see some of Cornwall's most breathtaking cliffscapes. Regardless of whether it's a calm or windy day, the views and atmosphere around here are always special, and there's a good chance you'll see seals basking on the rocks below.

Times past

Take a walk around the streets of Camborne, with its rows of small, terraced cottages built specifically to house a rapidly growing industrial population. In Redruth, look out for some of the grand civic buildings in the town centre, like the impressive Mining Exchange building.

Highlights

Cycle or walk along the Great Flat Lode trail, which, along its extent of just under four miles, has the highest concentration of historic mining sites anywhere in the world

Climb up to the Basset memorial on Carn Brea, which dominates the Area, and see the spectacular views from its summit

Visit East Pool Mine, and see the interiors of two complete engine houses with engines in situ. Explore mining models and hands on activities which explain how the mine worked

Walk along the headland at Portreath, and imagine the harbour in its industrial heyday as a bustling copper port

Explore Wheal Peevor, which has three fine engine houses close to the A30

Witness the unique collection of restored tin processing equipment at King Edward Mine, a former training centre for mining students dating from the turn of the 20th century—one of only a few remaining mine sites with extensive collections of machinery. The Croust Hut café on site serves Cornish food daily throughout the year

Head to Heartlands, Cornwall's first free cultural playground on a grand scale. Covering 19 acres with Diaspora themed botanical gardens, interactive exhibitions, an adventure playground, café and engine house, Heartlands hosts a diverse menu of events all year round. It is a cultural hub on what was once the richest patch of land on earth

Camborne industrial housing | Barry Gamble

06.
Gwennap

Gwennap Pit | Barry Gamble

Great cycle trails through
the Copper Kingdom

A large and varied Area of fertile countryside, historic mining villages, pretty woods, tranquil river creeks and some of the most impressive industrial landscapes to be found anywhere in the Site, Gwennap is full of contrasts. Once the richest of all Cornwall's mining districts, its fine houses, well-preserved industrial remains and dramatic, alien-looking mining landscapes combine to tell a compelling and colourful story of Cornish Mining's heyday. The Methodist preaching place Gwennap Pit, along with the Area's many roadside chapels, also give us a fascinating insight into mining communities and their spiritual beliefs.

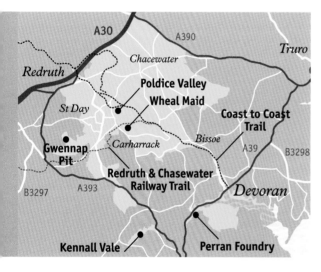

Portreath. At Poldice and Wheal Maid, the change wrought by mining and ore processing is profound, as extensive, vegetation-bare mine-dumps punctuate the landscape (although many host bryophytes—nationally important simple plant species).

In contrast, the site of the Kennall Vale Gunpowder Works, which produced explosives used to drive tunnels and remove ore, is now a tranquil woodland managed by Cornwall Wildlife Trust. Here, disused mills line the course of the Kennall River, once the source of power for grinding the gunpowder mixture. Perran Foundry, by the creek at Perran Wharf, was one of the world's most important Cornish engine manufacturers and ironfounders.

The settlements of St Day, Chacewater and Carharrack retain their individual identities and active community life. Their terraces and chapels are testimony to their mining origins, and remain an essential part of their character today.

Mining Heritage

This Area saw the early use of steam **beam engines** for pumping and some of the oldest **engine houses** to survive in Cornwall can be found here. Tramways – including two of Cornwall's earliest and most important – thread through this Area, linking its mines to the well-preserved ports of Devoran and

Practicalities

Getting there • This large Area lies between Redruth and Truro, and is laced with classic Cornish lanes. Road access is via the **A393** between Redruth and Falmouth, which passes through Ponsanooth (for Kennall Vale); turn off this road by the Fox & Hounds pub for Carharrack, St Day, Scorrier and Chacewater. **First bus 47** passes through Carharrack, St Day and Chacewater. Devoran is just off the **A39** between Falmouth and Truro, and First bus routes **U1/U2** (Falmouth to Truro) stop here. See **firstgroup.com/cornwall** for more information

Suggested map • **Ordnance Survey map 104**: Redruth & St Agnes (Explorer Maps)

Dog friendliness • This is a rural Area with lots of footpaths, and is generally great for dogs. Keep dogs on leads on farmland with grazing animals though, and refer to the signs at each site

Parking • The villages of St Day, Carharrack and Chacewater have limited on-street parking. The cycle hire shop and café at Bissoe also has free parking for hire customers

Public toilets • The cycle hire shop and café at Bissoe offers toilets

Eating & drinking • The Norway Inn at Perranarworthal and the Quay Inn at Devoran both have great menus featuring lots of local produce. The café at the Bissoe Cycle Hire centre has a warm welcome and a good selection of meals, cakes and snacks on offer. St Day and Chacewater both have good village pubs

Picnic spots • There are some nice benches and grassy spots by the river at Devoran, and lots of good places to stop if you're cycling along the Mineral Tramways Trail. Alternatively, find a relaxing spot next to one of the streams in the lovely woods at Kennall Vale. Please help us to look after the World Heritage Site by taking all rubbish away with you

Dubbed 'the Copper Kingdom of the Old World', Gwennap produced a major proportion of the world's copper supply in the 18th and 19th centuries.

Poldice Arsenic works | Barry Gamble

Did you know?
In the 19th century Gwennap was described as the 'richest square mile in the Old World'

49

Tailings lagoon in the Wheal Maid Valley | Barry Gamble

Discover...

Industry

Hire a bike at Bike Chain in Bissoe and cycle the Mineral Tramways Coast to Coast Trail, which links the principal mine sites, the eastern and western parts of this Area, and the important ports of Devoran and Portreath. The Redruth & Chasewater Railway Trail also links Bissoe with Redruth via Carharrack as part of this network.

Nature

Originally planted to absorb the blast damage from accidental explosions in the gunpowder works, the oak woodland at Kennall Vale is now an important nature reserve with rich undergrowth, open glades and a water-filled quarry. Look out for dippers (brown birds which hunt for their food in water).

Times past

Just to the south of Redruth on the eastern slopes of Carn Marth is the famous Gwennap Pit, where John Wesley is understood to have preached between 1762 and 1789. With its message of the rewards waiting in Heaven, Methodism was very popular with the hardworking mining communities. Wesley is known to have preached to many thousands at this location though the Pit's capacity was reduced to 1,500 when the tiers were installed in 1806.

Highlights

Cycle the stunning Mineral Tramways Coast to Coast Trail, which passes through some incredible mining landscapes. Level for most of the way (with the odd slight incline), enjoy the invigoration of cycling an almost 25 mile round trip in a day – from Devoran on the River Fal to the lovely harbour and beach at Portreath on the north coast, and back

Explore the Kennall Vale Gunpowder Works – one of the largest and most complete gunpowder works to be found anywhere in Britain – set in gorgeous woods laced with streams, leats, waterfalls and ponds. In spring, a sea of bluebells and bright pink foxgloves carpets the woodland floor

Stand in the famous Gwennap Pit, where John Wesley preached to the Cornish Mining communities, imagining thousands of people gathered around to listen to you

Take in the sheer scale of past industrial activity at Poldice and Wheal Maid, which reveal the enormous impact that mining has had in transforming the landscape of this part of Cornwall

Look around the well-preserved port, quays and tramway trackbeds at Devoran, once a key mining port and now a beautiful and tranquil creekside haven

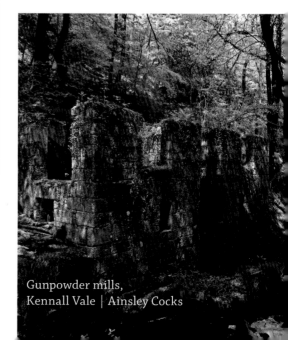

Gunpowder mills, Kennall Vale | Ainsley Cocks

07.
St Agnes

Towanroath Shaft pumping engine house, Wheal Coates, from Chapel Porth | Ainsley Cocks

Iconic cliff-top engine houses
and world-class tin

Famous for its spectacular coastline and well-preserved engine houses perched on rugged cliffs, this Area also has a rich heritage to explore inland – from the tin treatment works in narrow stream valleys to the pretty village with its granite mine workers' cottages, fine public buildings and luscious gardens. Come here for great walks, breathtaking sunsets, dramatic mining remains, stunning beaches and, if you're lucky, to see the dolphins that play off the coast in the summer.

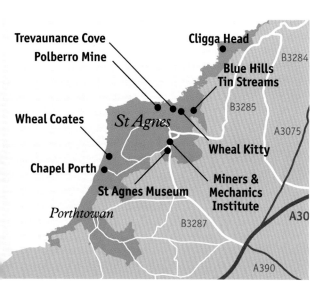

Trevaunance Cove
Polberro Mine
Cligga Head
B3284
Blue Hills Tin Streams
B3285
Wheal Coates
St Agnes
A3075
Chapel Porth
Wheal Kitty
St Agnes Museum
Miners & Mechanics Institute
Porthtowan
A30
B3287
A390

Mining Heritage

St Agnes reflects the influence of mining on the settlement, with its shops, pubs, hotels, chapels and public buildings like the Miners and Mechanics Institute (built to serve a growing population employed in the industry). At Trevaunance Cove, you'll see the remnants of an old harbour, from where local copper ore was taken to South Wales. Frequently battered by Atlantic storms, this harbour had to be rebuilt four times before finally succumbing to the sea during the early 20th century.

Inland, to the south and east, you'll see many well-preserved smallholdings. You can also watch tin being crushed and separated at the fascinating restored Blue Hills Tin Streams in Trevellas Coombe. Walk the coast path to Cligga Head to see the dramatic influence of mining on the coastline here.

At high tide, the waves crash against the rocks below the open mine shaft at Wheal Coates, while seabirds circle and dive in the sea air, making their nests on the cliffs

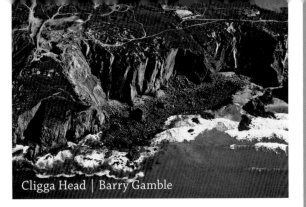
Cligga Head | Barry Gamble

Practicalities

Getting there • By car, St Agnes is easily accessible from the **A30 via the B3277**, and is roughly nine miles from Truro. By bus, the **First 87** runs from Truro regularly during the week. See **firstgroup.com/cornwall** for more information

Suggested map • **Ordnance Survey map 104**: Redruth & St Agnes (Explorer Maps)

Dog friendliness • Trevaunance Cove and Trevellas Porth both allow dogs all year round. All dogs (except guide dogs) are banned from Chapel Porth and Porthtowan beaches from Easter Day to 1st October

Parking • The main car park is in the village centre (next to the library), and there are also car parks at Wheal Kitty and the four main beaches

Public toilets • There are public toilets in the car parks of Chapel Porth, Porthtowan and Trevaunance Cove, as well as in the main village car park

Eating & drinking • Schooners, The St Agnes Hotel, The Tap House, and The Driftwood Spars all offer great food and drink and a warm welcome, or grab a freshly-made pasty from the fantastic St Agnes Bakery (they even have a vegan pasty) and head for the great outdoors. The café at Chapel Porth is home of the legendary 'Hedgehog' ice cream (a must!), and at Porthtowan the Blue Bar and Beach Café are both popular venues right by the beach

Picnic spots • Too many to mention! The coastal path that runs all along this Area has hundreds of spectacular spots to sit and take it all in. Please help us to look after the World Heritage Site by taking all rubbish away with you

The tin found in this Area was known to be of a very high quality. Mining started here hundreds of years before the copper and tin boom of the 18th and 19th centuries, when the cliffs and valleys clattered with the noise of continuous production. Although Polberro Mine was to reach its height in the 1800s, it had long been operating as one of the largest and richest tin mines in Cornwall. So much tin ore was produced there in 1750 that it is said there were insufficient pack horses locally to transport it to the smelters.

Towanroath Shaft pumping engine house, Wheal Coates | Ainsley Cocks

Wheal Coates Whim and Stamps engine houses | Ainsley Cocks

Discover...

Mining

Follow the mining trail beginning at the famous Wheal Coates tin mine on the cliffs near Chapel Porth, passing the old workings at Polberro and Wheal Kitty, and ending at Blue Hills at Trevellas.

Nature

When walking the coast path, look out for peregrine falcons, which nest on many of the headlands. Gannets can usually be seen flying low over the sea a few hundred yards from the coast.

Times past

Park at the top of the village (by the library), visit the nearby St Agnes Museum, then walk down past the Miners and Mechanics Institute, St Agnes church, the St Agnes Hotel, and the famous Stippy Stappy cottages (built for ships' captains sailing from Trevaunance Cove), following the path down to the old harbour.

Highlights

Walk around the stunning cliff-top engine house at Wheal Coates: pictured on hundreds of postcards, but must be seen for real

Visit the site of the old harbour at Trevaunance Cove, now in ruins, with a lovely beach and some great eateries

Explore the lively and historic village of St Agnes, with its pubs, cafés and pretty rows of granite cottages like Stippy Stappy

Walk the stark coastline around Cligga Head, world famous for its outstanding mineralogy and cliff workings

Surf the coastline between Porthtowan and Trevaunance Cove – or go walking and kite-flying on the golden sands

Visit St Agnes Museum to discover more about the Area's mining heritage

Did you know?
Tin-plated iron and later steel cans changed food storage forever

St Agnes Museum | Emma Parkman

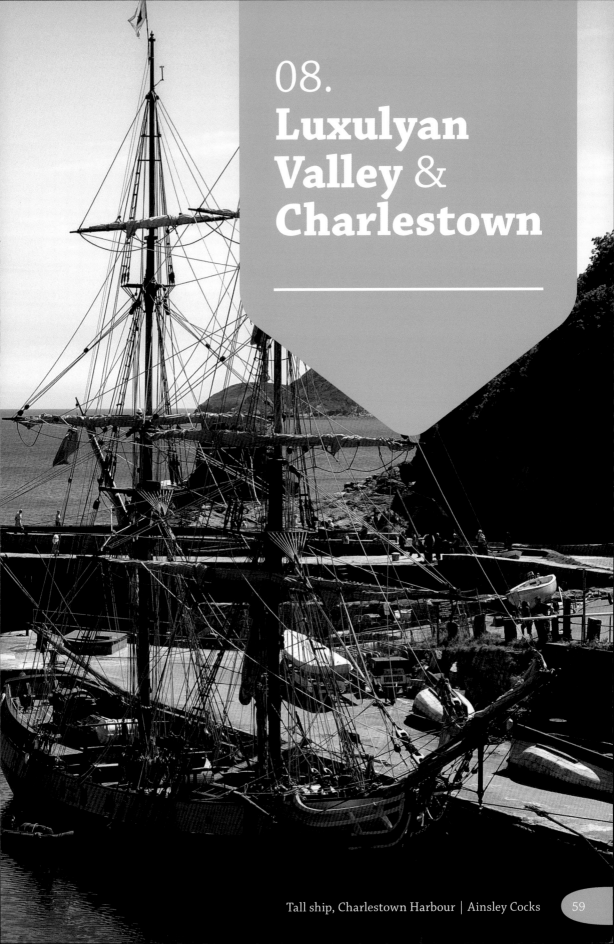

08.
Luxulyan Valley & Charlestown

The creations of two
extraordinary industrialists

From tranquil green woods to a bustling harbour village, the landscapes of the Luxulyan Valley and Charlestown are very different. However, they share important similarities: both are stunningly beautiful places with rich mining histories to explore and both were created by two locally-prominent industrial entrepreneurs. Charlestown, whose picturesque harbour has featured in many films, was developed in the late 18th century by Charles Rashleigh, while many of the industrial works within the Luxulyan Valley – including the Treffry Viaduct, leats and tramways – were constructed by Joseph Treffry during the early to mid-1800s.

Mining Heritage

Water was crucial to both locations in this Area. Charlestown Harbour was built between 1792 and 1801, and is today the best preserved copper ore and china-clay shipping port of its period anywhere in the world. The new harbour required a reliable water source to both fill the dock and flush out accumulated silt. To achieve this a seven-mile leat was constructed to a point on the Par River, near the head of the Luxulyan Valley. By 1850 Charlestown was well established as an industrial village with its own tin smelter and foundry, requiring the harbour to be enlarged towards the end of the century due to ships overcrowding the original dock.

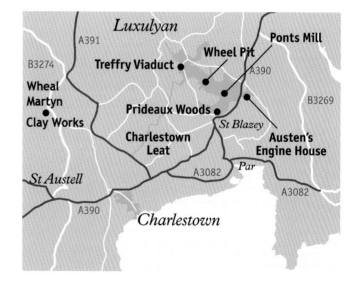

The timid shrills of bats can sometimes be heard around the mines in Prideaux Woods

Practicalities

Getting there • Charlestown is just 2 miles south from St Austell. Luxulyan is a five mile drive northeast of St Austell along some narrow but well signposted roads. First operates several buses to St Austell **(21, 22, 24, 25, 27)**, and the **101** from St Austell stops in Luxulyan. See **firstgroup.com/cornwall** for timetables. The nearest mainline train station is **Par**. See **nationalrail.co.uk** for the latest information

Suggested map • **Ordnance Survey map 107**: St Austell & Liskeard, Fowey, Looe & Lostwithiel (Explorer Maps)

Dog friendliness • There are some excellent walks around the Treffry Viaduct and the Luxulyan Valley, but dogs are banned on the beach at Charlestown all year round

Parking • The pay car park in Charlestown is a short walk from the harbour. At Luxulyan Valley there are 2 small car parks at Black Hill and Ponts Mill

Public toilets • There are toilets at Luxulyan Museum and Heritage Centre (open Tuesdays to Saturdays in the summer school holidays – or call 01726 813522 to arrange visits at other times)

Eating & drinking • Charlestown has a great range of food and drink - Charlie's Coffee House offers lovely coffee and cake. The Rashleigh Arms, The Longstore and Wreckers all serve good local food. The Pier House, also in Charlestown, serves great meals with a harbour view. In Luxulyan, The Kings Arms is a lovely traditional pub serving real ale and good food. Wheal Martyn Clay works, St Austell also has a cosy, welcoming café

Picnic spots • Around Luxulyan, there are benches and walls that you can perch on along the various woodland walks that take in the viaduct, canal and leats. At Charlestown, you can either stop at the beach, or walk the cliff path up to Charlestown Battery, which was built by Charles Rashleigh to defend the harbour during the Napoleonic Wars. Please help us to look after the World Heritage Site by taking all rubbish away with you

Features within and around the Luxulyan Valley include a three mile leat constructed to power the many water wheels and water pressure engines at Fowey Consols Mine; a canal to take its copper ore to the purpose-built harbour at Par; and a horse-drawn tramway to provide a link to the mines of the hinterland and give access to the granite quarries at nearby Colcerrow. The most impressive feature within the Valley is undoubtedly the Treffry Viaduct, the imposing granite structure which carries both a leat and tramway route high above the Valley floor.

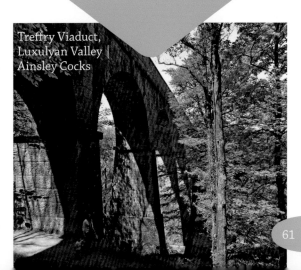

Treffry Viaduct, Luxulyan Valley | Ainsley Cocks

Discover...

Mining

Visit Wheal Martyn Clay Works at nearby Carthew, St Austell, which tells the story of extractive industries in this Area since the decline of tin and copper mining. Gaze hundreds of feet down into the neighbouring working modern day china clay pit from the special viewing platform. See the Waterwheels, The Wagon Huts and the indoor discovery centre, or explore the acres of woodland walks and nature trails.

Nature

Walk along the valley woodland near to Ponts Mill and be enchanted by the springs and streams, wildflowers, birds and winding paths. Many different ferns, mosses and lichens add vibrancy to this Area.

Times past

Stand atop the imposing granite structure of the Treffry Viaduct (completed in 1842 to carry water and a tramway), and take in the birds-eye view of this beautiful valley.

Highlights

Stand under the Treffry Viaduct, which – despite being huge – manages to hide itself among the woodland until it is literally upon you!

Walk the attractive circular route from Ponts Mill along Par Canal (90 minutes), which was created to transport copper ore from Fowey Consols to Par Harbour

Glimpse Austen's Engine House above Penpillick, part of the Fowey Consols copper mine

The huge water wheel pit on the valley side near Carmears Rocks shows the sheer scale of operations here

Experience the delightful Prideaux Woods (to the south-west of Luxulyan Valley) – a quarter of which is ancient woodland

Visit Charlestown Harbour and view the historic wharves

Did you know?
The 80 inch cylinder pumping engine formerly at Fowey Consols Mine was the most efficient ever recorded

Austens Engine House, Fowey Consols | Ainsley Cocks

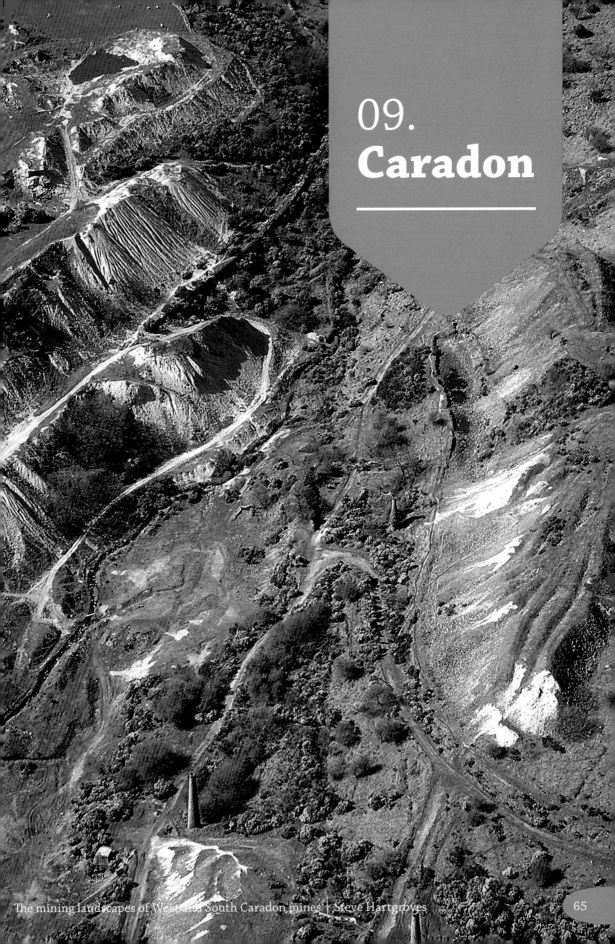

09.
Caradon

Boom to bust mining amongst rugged moorland

This rugged, windswept and mostly treeless Area sits high up in a remote but beautiful corner of Bodmin Moor. Rising dramatically from the surrounding plain, the granite dome of Caradon Hill dominates the Area and is encircled by engine houses, chimney stacks, thousands of tonnes of waste rock from the various mines and quarries, and the trackbed of the Liskeard and Caradon Railway. This is a story of boom and bust: the rise of copper mining here established new settlements and expanded others, but the explosion of mining activity within this formerly isolated landscape was to last barely 50 years; large-scale mining for copper had essentially ceased by 1890.

Caradon's mining landscape is defined by wide open spaces

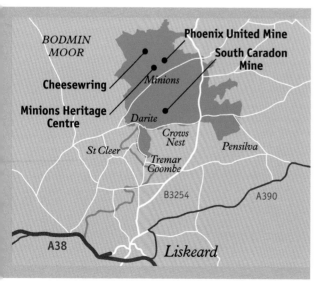

Mining Heritage

In Cornish mining terms, this Area was a late starter. Although it had a long history of tin streaming and shallow mining, it was the copper riches discovered at South Caradon Mine in 1836 that sparked a huge mining boom and the rapid development of the Caradon Mining District. Unusually, the copper found here was within the granite of Caradon Hill, giving the Area international mineralogical significance.

Operated from 1836 to the late 1880s, the whole process from discovery to final closure barely lasted half a century. During this time, railways, tramways, mines, roads and quarries were built, and the previously sparsely populated moorland hosted thousands of mine workers and their families, who were to live in new or greatly expanded settlements of terraced cottages, chapels and schools (e.g. Darite, Pensilva and Minions, the latter formerly known as Cheesewring Railway).

Practicalities

Getting there • By car, turn off the **A38** at Liskeard and follow the St Cleer road up onto the moors. From the **A30**, turn off at South Petherwin. **Plymouth Citybus** operate the **74** and **174** routes linking Liskeard with St Cleer and The Crow's Nest Inn, next to South Caradon mine. Visit **plymouthbus.co.uk** for timetables. The nearest mainline train station is **Liskeard**. See **nationalrail.co.uk** for the latest information

Suggested map • **Ordnance Survey map 109**: Bodmin Moor: Bodmin, Camelford and Liskeard (Explorer Series Active Map)

Moorland • Keep to the Bodmin Moor Code of Conduct for visitors, which is displayed in the car parks

Dog friendliness • Please keep dogs on a lead where sheep, cattle or ponies are grazing, and at all times between 1 March - 31 July

Parking • There is ample parking in Minions, by the Minions Heritage Centre. There is a car park south of Minions, near the Hurlers

Public toilets • There are public toilets in Liskeard's main carpark

Eating & drinking • The Hurlers' Halt and the Post Office serve good traditional cream teas in an atmospheric setting, and the Manor House Country Inn and Restaurant at Rilla Mill is a quality modern eatery in a restored country inn. The Crows Nest Inn is also a traditional cosy pub serving good local food close to South Caradon Mine

Picnic spots • The Cheesewring is a famous stack of giant, flat boulders balanced in a striking setting high up on the moors. Close by, The Hurlers is a line of three giant stone circles, said to be Cornish men turned to stone by St Cleer for playing a game of hurling on a Sunday when they should have been at church. The whole landscape is steeped in history with fantastic views in every direction. Please help us to look after the World Heritage Site by taking all rubbish away with you

In the late 1800s men from the declining mines in other parts of Cornwall flocked to the district, but left as soon as the mines closed, leaving it almost empty once again. However, the Area's remote location has ensured the exceptional survival of its mining heritage.

Holman's and Rule's Engine Houses, South Caradon Mine | Barry Gamble

Prince of Wales Shaft Engine House, Phoenix United Mine | Barry Gamble

Discover...

Mining

Walk along the disused railways, tramroads and traction engine tracks across the moorland, which form well-surfaced level trails through the Area. These routes link some of the richest and best-preserved archaeological landscapes in Cornwall, including South Caradon Mine, the Prince of Wales shaft site (Phoenix United Mine), the Hurlers, and Cheesewring Quarry.

Nature

Take a walk around the Cheesewring rock formation, which has been carved out by the powerful forces of nature. Formed during the Ice Ages, its distinctive shape has been sculpted by the elements that battered this exposed location for thousands of years. If you're lucky, you'll also see moorland ponies and skylarks, as well as heather and wildflowers.

Times past

Explore the village of Minions – Cornwall's highest village – which has the feel of a real frontier settlement, with rows of terraced cottages built up on the virgin moorland. Learn more about its history in the Minions Heritage Centre, which is kindly managed by volunteers and although open most days can be locked when volunteers are unavailable.

Highlights

Walk on open access land along the old Liskeard & Caradon Railway (built to transport copper-ore southwards to the port of Looe), with its mostly level surface, stunning views and striking reminders of its industrial past

Watch the sunset from the top of Caradon Hill, looking west across the golden moors and Siblyback Lake

Visiting the Prince of Wales Shaft at Phoenix United Mine, built for the last big pumping engine made in Cornwall (1907). It's an impressive and distinctive landmark with great views across the countryside. Nearby, the Houseman's engine house, part of South Phoenix Mine, is now partially restored as the Minions Heritage Centre, it is kindly managed by volunteers so is open most days but relies on volunteers availability —well worth a visit either way as the building from the exterior is quite impressive

Explore the well-preserved cobbled floors of South Caradon Mine at the bottom of the Seaton Valley where many women and children worked to dress (process) copper ore. The towering bleached white waste dumps either side are a striking testament to the scale of operations beneath this moorland landscape

Visit Liskeard Museum to discover more about the Area's heritage

Did you know?

Copper mining at Caradon brought thousands of mine workers to the district almost overnight

Bellingham's Shaft pumping engine house, Wheal Jenkin | Ainsley Cocks

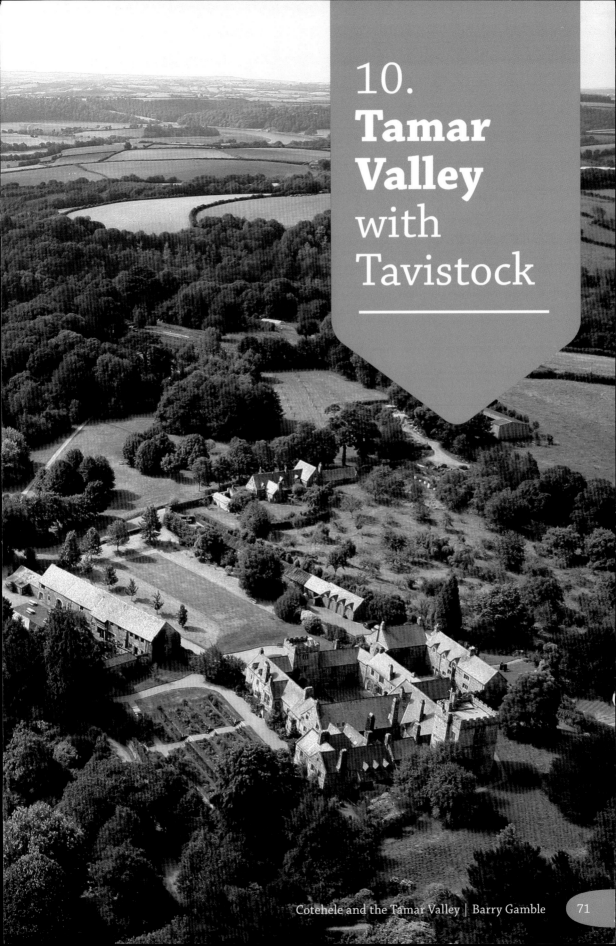

10.
Tamar Valley
with Tavistock

Nature and history **entwined**

Set in an Area of Outstanding Natural Beauty (AONB), the Tamar Valley encompasses a breathtaking landscape that is as diverse as it is historically important. Stretching from the high granite ridge and exposed moors of Kit Hill in Cornwall to the lush, deep wooded valleys of the meandering Tamar River – and the farming lands of the Devon plateau beyond – the Area spans the border between Cornwall and Devon. In today's tranquillity, it's hard to imagine the noise from over 100 mines that operated at the height of its mining boom.

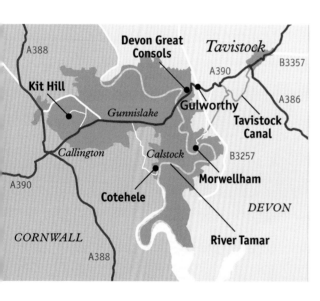

Arsenic chimney, Devon Great Consols Mine | Barry Gamble

Mining Heritage

Tin, copper, silver-lead, and arsenic were all mined here. The steep valley sides exposed lode outcrops, so many of the Area's mines are sited on the sheer wooded slopes running down to the river. In places, engine houses and associated buildings are well preserved; elsewhere you'll glimpse an occasional chimney or fragment of walling emerging through the trees.

Devon Great Consols and Gawton mine were supplying half of the world's arsenic by the end of the 19th century. Today, their waste dumps, the leaning Gawton chimney stack and remains of the flues and arsenic refinery are impressive. On the Bere Alston peninsula (west Devon) are some of the only true silver mines in Britain, first worked in the early 13th century.

Cotehele Quay | Barry Gamble

Practicalities

Getting there • By car, the **A390** crosses the Area, across Hingston Down and Gunnislake to Tavistock. A good selection of ferry, bus and train services run from Plymouth through the Tamar Valley Area. Visit **tamarvalley.org.uk** and **plymouthboattrips.co.uk** for more information

Suggested map • **Ordnance Survey map 108**: Lower Tamar Valley & Plymouth, Tavistock and Callington (Explorer Series)

Dog friendliness • The Tamar Valley has a good network of footpaths and trails, including the Tamar Valley Discovery Trail. Please remember to keep your dog on a lead in the wildlife reserve areas

Parking • There are car parks at Gunnislake, Tavistock, Kit Hill, Calstock and Morwellham Quay

Public toilets • These can be found in Gunnislake, Calstock and Morwellham Quay

Eating & drinking • The Boot Inn at Calstock has a great menu that is a cut above your average pub grub. Cothele has two lovely cafés, and you can also make the most of the Tamar Valley Rail Ale Trail scheme, which encourages rail travellers to visit pubs near the line, see **greatscenicrailways. co.uk/rail-ale-trails** for more information. Bere Ferrers and Bere Alston each have a pub on the scheme; there is one in Calstock and five in Gunnislake. Louis' Tea Rooms, right by the entrance to Kit Hill Country Park, offers hot food, cakes and cream teas. Tavistock has lots of good cafés and shops

Picnic spots • On a clear sunny day, the view from Kit Hill takes some beating. There are also lots of scenic, peaceful quays along the river's edge at places like Halton Quay, Weir Quay and Cotehele. Please help us to look after the World Heritage Site by taking all rubbish away with you

There is an exceptional mineral transport network here: you'll find an unparalleled group of industrial mineral river quays (e.g. Morwellham), a mine railway (which served Devon Great Consols), a mineral railway (East Cornwall Mineral Railway), and a mineral canal (Tavistock Canal). The Area also has numerous mine quays, mule tracks and mine roads, many of which have now been opened up as multi-use trails for visitors.

Okel Tor Mine | Ainsley Cocks

Discover...

Mining

Join the Tamar Valley Discovery Trail at New Bridge, and follow the route along to Gunnislake Clitters Mine where substantial engine houses stand close to the river and further up the hill. The Discovery Trail also connects a number of other key industrial sites.

Nature

Take a boat trip on the river – a fantastic opportunity to see the range of bird, fish and insect life that thrive here. Look out for salmon, heron, kingfisher, ducks and swans. You can also explore the Tamar Valley Wildlife Reserve at Morwellham Quay, which covers over 200 acres.

Times past

Visit Morwellham Quay. Explore the quay, mine and farm cottages, school and shops of 1860; watch craftsmen at work; and travel along the 1500ft underground mine train into a copper mine to experience what it was like for mine workers of the time.

Highlights

Visit the Tamar Trails Centre and walk or cycle the wooded trails around Devon Great Consols, one of the largest and most important copper and arsenic works in the Site. **www.tamartrails.co.uk**

Explore the shops, cafés, elegant houses and villas, public buildings and museum in the historic former mining town of Tavistock - extensively re-modelled in the 19th century by the 7th Duke of Bedford

Ride the train on the Tamar Valley Line – the southern section of the former East Cornwall Minerals Railway. This runs through the Tamar Valley's breathtaking scenery, over the stunning Tavy and Calstock viaducts, and through some of the key mining sites and communities

Gaze out across the magnificent panoramas from the top of Kit Hill. Look northwards across the sweeping landscape of north Cornwall and north Devon; southwards across rich farmland to the waters of Plymouth Haven shining in the distance; or westwards towards Caradon Hill and Bodmin Moor crowning the horizon

Discover the magical house, gardens, woodlands, riverside walks and quays of Cotehele, the historic seat of the Edgcumbe family

> **Did you know?**
> *Francis Russell the 7th Duke of Bedford (1788-1861) reputedly earned over £2 million (some £178 million today) from his mineral interests in the Tamar Valley*

Bedford Square, Tavistock | Ainsley Cocks